Faith Bigger Than Me

Abigail Judith Hall

DEDICATION

To my children, whom have been the instruments by which God has taught me great faith. You boys are the manifestation of God's strength and goodness.

Introduction:

How exciting that you've decided to embark on a journey with the goal of building your faith! Who can't use a boost in the faith department, right? I pray before and as I write this that this will be an absolutely life-altering experience. Sounds like a lot to ask from a daily devotional, but truthfully, it's all about you; and what perspective you enter into this with. If you really and truly want to grow your faith, I promise you, you will. So, before you start, ask yourself some questions.

Question number one: Do you want this? Do you really want to see your faith grow bigger than you? If you can honestly say yes, they answer the next question.

Question number two: Why? Why do you want stronger faith? I realize many of you may think, "Duh! We all need faith!" To that I say, yes, but *why*? Think about this. Reflect on it. What part does faith play in your life? Is there a goal you're after? Be honest with yourself. Do you want stronger faith so you can see a certain miracle happen in your life? Do you want stronger faith because you doubt your beliefs? Do you feel powerless? Do you simply feel like you need to be a better Christian? Maybe you're doing okay, but you feel like you need to challenge yourself. When you identify your answer, write it down! Know what it is you're really chasing. Trust me, it matters.

The next question is an extension of the last one. Question number three: How will your life change if your faith grows?
Please, take the time to really answer these questions. Then pray over them. Ask the Lord to open your heart and the eyes of your spirit to see and hear what He wants to say to you. No journey is worth beginning without Him.

Day 1: Why Faith?

There is no possible way I could tell you the number of sermons or lessons I've heard or read on faith. If you've spent any time in church, my bet is that your experience has been much the same. Faith is a headliner topic.

With such an emphasis on faith, it begs the question: why? You'll remember this is one of the questions I asked in the introduction. Why do *you* want faith? I sincerely hope you answered that question. We know we need faith, but before we can build great faith, we desperately need to understand *why* we need it.

Some may say it's because they want to see miracles. Great! Some may say they want the power of God. Great! Some may say they want to overcome doubt. Great! Some may say they want to be challenged in their walk. Great! All of those are fantastic, but here is the real deal: those are all by-products of great faith, not the goal. Great faith is important, not because you can achieve great things spiritually; but because faith solidifies your place in Christ. Let me unpack that for you. We are asked, commanded, and pleaded with throughout scripture to have faith. Why? Because your level of faith is a direct reflection of your understanding, love, and devotion to God Himself. If you understand Who He is even just a little, your faith will reflect it. If you love Him, even just a little bit, your faith will show it. If you are devoted to Him, it will be unmistakable in your faith. Without faith, can you even know Him? The answer is no. You see, grace is the door you walk through to get to Him, but faith is the key that unlocks it.

The answer to why faith is important is that everything about your walk with Jesus is built on it. The more it grows, the more your relationship with Him grows. To go a bit further, I dare say that your relationship with the Lord cannot grow without your faith growing in some measure, and vice versa. They are tethered to one another. The more you love someone and grow nearer to them, the more you entrust to them and the more you open yourself up to them. The Lord wants to be intimately acquainted with you, and that requires faith enough to walk with Him, wherever He wants to take you. How can He possibly rendezvous with you if you don't trust Him to take you anywhere? If you are a seasoned Christian and you trust Him greatly, ask yourself how much deeper He can take you if you learn to have even deeper faith?

So, in summary, why faith? Because it's your passageway into a greater love affair with the One who thought you were worth His own life.

"But without faith, it is impossible to [walk with God and] please Him, for whoever comes [near] to God must [necessarily] believe that God exists and that He rewards those who [earnestly and diligently] seek Him."
Hebrews 11:6 (AMP)

Reflection and Prayer Focus

Today, I challenge you to read the entire chapter of Hebrews 11 and consider it in the light of today's devotional thoughts. Do you see how the examples of those who honored God with their faith were actually just reflecting their own love and devotion toward Him? If someone were to write about you in this context, what would be the picture they have of your faith? Being brutally honest, what would it imply about your love and devotion to God? Based on the displays of faith in your life, is your love for God fierce?

During your prayer time today, spend time asking God to show you how you do or don't love Him fiercely. Ask Him to help you see Him for Who He is because once you know Who He is, you'll be unable to do anything but love Him, or love Him more.

Personal Notes

Day 2: What is Faith?

Yesterday we questioned why we want/need faith. I hope you took the time to pray and reflect on this question. I truly hope this got your wheels turning and meditating on this idea of faith. We are barely scratching the surface right now. You see, you can't actually understand the full why until you answer the what.

What is faith? You might say, "it's trusting God." Yes! It really is that simple, and yet it's not remotely that bland. Faith is a continuous exercise of level after level of trusting God. Eventually, the goal is to walk so deeply in faith that you reflect far more of Him than you do of yourself.

To discuss the what of faith is going to span more than a day. This is just our starting place. Let me hit you with something kind of deep to ponder. Most of us who have spent much time in church or reading the Bible know the scripture Hebrews 11:1. It begins with the words, "Faith is the substance of things hoped for, the evidence of things not seen." I am not going on a mission to rewrite this passage, but I am on a mission to reframe the way you think about faith. We tend to read this passage and absorb it as the thought that faith is the essence of the impossible. It is made manifest in miracles; and it is actively at work in the things we have *yet* to see, but will, with enough disciplined belief.

Go with me for a minute as we look at it through a slightly different lens. What if you start to think about faith as being the cord that connects you to the current of God's power. Every answered prayer you've prayed, and every good thing you have seen in your life is "the substance of things hoped for." Let it remind you that it is by faith that you've seen God's hand at work in your life. It is by faith in His great power that you've not only had needs met, but you've seen healings, miracles, and the unexplainable things that you've hoped for come to be things of substance! Look at the job you believed God for. Substance. Look at the clean bill of health you believed God for. Substance. Look at the open doors you had no way of opening. Substance. Look at the reconciled relationships in your life that were broken beyond repair. Substance. The things of substance in your life are the direct product of putting your faith in the Lord.

Now, let's consider that second part, "the evidence of things not seen." What if you start to think about faith as being such an immovable way of thinking, acting, and living, that this passage morphs into a new mentality. What if it stops being about the things you're going to strong-arm God into giving you because He can't ignore your faith? Consider this: faith is evident *even when* the miracle is not present. Faith is active *even when* the healing doesn't come. Faith is strong, *even when* the prayer is answered with a no. This is not about impressing God with your faith so much that He gives you whatever you want. It is about having such deep faith in Him that *nothing* phases it. It's not necessarily the evidence of things God will give you because you believe. It has to be about having the kind of faith that does not waver when things are not seen.

What is faith? It's an unrelenting commitment to the One Who gave Himself for you, all the way to death, with unrelenting love.

"Now faith is the substance of things hoped for, the evidence of things not seen. For by it the elders obtained a good testimony. By faith we understand that the worlds were framed by the word of God, so that the things which are seen were not made of things which are visible."
Hebrews 11:1 (NKJV)

Reflection and Prayer Focus

Today, spend time thanking Jesus for His incredible sacrifice. Do it thoroughly. Don't just say thank you. Stop and thank Him for every pain He felt, every rip in His flesh, every tear He cried. Fall in love with His unyielding and wildly passionate devotion to you. Ask Him to help you devote yourself to Him the way He has done for you. This is where unwavering faith is born.

14

Personal Notes

_____

_____

_____

_____

_____

_____

_____

_____

_____

_____

_____

_____

_____

_____

_____

_____

_____

_____

_____

_____

_____

_____

_____

Day 3: What Faith Looks Like

Hopefully, your thoughts on faith are already being challenged. I sincerely hope you are seeking God at every turn through this study. After diving right in the last couple of days and discussing why we need faith and what it is, let's consider what it looks like.

You've probably heard that Love is an action verb. I always love this. Now, here is something else to consider; what would happen in your life if you started to live in such a way that love and faith were both action verbs for you? Let's take that a step further, I'm going to say something a little hard to swallow. You cannot have effective faith in the Lord without love. You also cannot love Him passionately without developing faith! As we established earlier, the two are connected. You can't have the kind of powerful, mountain-moving faith you're after if you're not crazy in love with Jesus. You cannot place real and meaningful faith in someone you don't love intimately and deeply.

Faith looks like love. Find out Who you're walking with and you will find yourself in love. The faith begins to grow when you choose Jesus. To keep it growing, you have to keep choosing Him. Daily. Under every circumstance. When things are going well, give Him the credit and praise. When things are going terribly, praise Him, and choose Him, even though you don't understand what is happening.

My faith has been challenged many times over the years. There have been so many times when I had no great inspiring words or incredible moments of my spirit rising up out of grand emotions. It was simply trudging through the muck and mire, determined to choose Jesus, no matter what. Some might use the word discipline. I prefer the word devotion. I am many things, a failure often being one of them. Yet, my devotion to Jesus is something I fight to my end for. The reason? I know Who He is. I know the places He's found me. I know the dark moments He has rescued me from. I know every disgusting failure of my life, every poor decision, every battle of depression and pain. He knows all of them too. He was there for all of them. I fail, and I fail often, including in my walk with the Lord, but I always find Him waiting for me, holding out his hand to pick me up again. That is why I keep returning. He has endured my pain with me, and even for me, over and over again. How can I not love Him? How can I not devote myself to someone so devoted to me?

That is what faith looks like. It looks like devotion to the love of your life. It's not aggressive, *demanding* anything, least of all miracles. It is not passive, or *accepting* of everything, least of all the attacks of the enemy. It is active, trusting the One Who fights alongside you, knowing that you will defeat the enemy, but there will be times things look bleak and you might endure some battle wounds. Even Jesus has scars. He is still victorious.

"I have loved you with an everlasting love; therefore, I have continued to extend faithful love to you."
Jeremiah 31:3 (CSB)

Reflection and Prayer Focus

In preparation for moving forward, ask the Lord to reveal your level of devotion to Him. Is it weak or strong? Are you ready to face trials and trust Him when things don't look so great? Ask Him to help you focus on Him and all of His goodness, not the circumstances around you. To be honest, every faith journey comes with a hefty dose of challenge. Ask Him to prepare you.

Personal Notes

Day 4: Unconditional Faith

We've kind of touched on the idea of faith no matter what, but I want to focus on this and drive it home a bit more. If you're really serious about building your faith, you are going to be fought by a real enemy. One that doesn't want you to grow closer to the Lord and doesn't want you to have stronger faith. That means you're going to endure some difficult attacks on your faith.

A few years ago, I became very aware of my own faith journey. My husband had just returned a few months earlier from his year-long military deployment in the Middle East. We had just learned we were expecting our first addition to our family. We later learned it was two additions. I had been pregnant with twins. We announced early because I had no fear. I even had people ask me if I was sure I wanted to tell the news so early since so many pregnancies are lost in the early weeks. I was appalled. This would never happen to me. It couldn't...because I trusted God. Our first couple of ultrasounds revealed very little. It was about the third one, which happened on Valentine's Day, that the doctor revealed that the lack of heartbeat meant the pregnancy was "not viable," and that we would, or rather had already lost the babies we so eagerly celebrated. I would have to wait for my body to get the memo and "clean things out." To say we were devastated would be underselling it. Everything inside of me hurt. I carried my already dead children, waiting for my body to release them. I grieved and ached. I questioned. I mourned. It was then that I began to learn that faith is often the hardest road. I had told people I had faith in the early days when I was aglow with pregnancy. God would protect my children. What about now?

I recall very vividly being told not to "lose faith," because God could do a miracle. I also recall my response, "I know God is able to do a miracle. Maybe He will. But for me, the biggest act of faith I have to offer Him right now is not believing for a miracle. It's choosing to believe that He is still Who He says He is, and He is still good, no matter what."

This is faith. It is sometimes painful and unpopular. Some might think it's weak not to demand a different set of circumstances. Faith is about being able to change things and move mountains, right? No. It's about believing the One Who made those mountains. Sometimes they are meant to be moved. Sometimes, we simply don't understand our circumstances and must rely on His goodness. This isn't weakness. It takes a great amount of faith to submit to His plan, even when it doesn't look like you think it should. Let me be clear that there is a time to stand your ground and move those mountains, but even then, it should always be with an attitude of submission to Him. He sees what you cannot see, and He knows what you cannot know. Trust Him, even when it looks weak. Trust Him, even when you feel hurt. Trust Him, even when you can't see Him. Remember that no matter what, He is everything He claims to be, and He loves you the way He has promised.

"My thoughts are nothing like your thoughts,' says the Lord. 'And my ways are far beyond anything you could imagine. For just as the heavens are higher than the earth, so my ways are higher than your ways and my thoughts higher than your thoughts."
Isaiah 55:8-9 (NLT)

Reflection and Prayer Focus

In your prayer time today, list the ways God has been faithful to you. Thank Him for each of them, and ask Him for the courage to be consistent in trusting Him. Remember that even when things look bad, He is on your side, and He wants desperately to be intimate with you.

Personal Notes

Day 5: Faithful Friend

When it comes to trusting God in the hard moments, the key to this is knowing Him. It's knowing the history of His faithfulness. In Deuteronomy 6, God instructs the Israelites to write down the things He has done for them, to keep a record, to recite them to their children, to wear them on their person. In Joshua 4, the Lord instructs them to put twelve stones of monuments in the Jordan River to commemorate that He had led them through it on dry land. Monuments and markers like this are a common theme in the Bible. They are incredibly important. Why? Because they cause us to remember. When your life is marked by victories, you cannot let a defeat destroy you. When memories of the lessons and goodness of God are sprinkled everywhere, you cannot believe He would fail you. When the Word of God and the promises He has made you are written on your heart, you will cling to them with all of your might.

You must keep a record of God's faithfulness so that you will never be a victim to the lies that He has failed you. There will be moments when the enemy whispers this to you. You must be able to counter with the list and recollections of all of the proof otherwise. Knowing His faithfulness makes you hyper-aware of His love and devotion to you. This matters! When the trials come, you're going to need to remember that He loves you, and He has proven it, time, and time again.

When it comes to your own faith, you can know that your faith in Him is not displaced. You will see incredible things, just like the Israelites, when you put your faith in Him. The miracles *will* happen. But you must remember that your faith can never be based on miracles. It must always be placed on Him. Real faith is about trusting God, not a set of circumstances or an expected outcome. You have to know He is trustworthy, no matter what. The miracles are definitely present with great faith, but believe me, moving the mountain has very little to do with believing the mountain will move. It has very much to do with believing in the faithfulness of the God Who made the mountain. If you have a relationship with Him, you are given some of His authority to see it move. If you don't have intimacy with Him, how can you seriously expect to have the authority to call miracles into existence? You can absolutely see the miracles if you first see Him, the faithful friend.

He has always been faithful to you, He has always chosen you. Will you choose Him? Will you revive the simple purity of trusting in Him every single day? Don't ever think you move past this stage in your walk with Him. You never can. It must be consistent.

"The Lord passed before him and proclaimed, 'The Lord, the Lord, a God merciful and gracious, slow to anger, and abounding in steadfast love and faithfulness..."
Exodus 34:6 (NRSV)

Reflection and Prayer Focus

Going forward, question your own motives in serving the Lord. Do you do it because you love Him passionately, or is it because you're supposed to? Is it because He is God, but there is no personal attachment to Him? Pray the Lord will reveal your own heart to you, get to the bottom of why you follow Him. Then ask Him to fill you with an undying passion for Him. He's coming for you. He's crazy enough to endure anything for you.

Personal Notes

Day 6: Withstanding Torture

Let's start out with intense today. Picture yourself in a nightmarish situation where you and the love of your life are dragged away from each other and locked in separate rooms to be tortured until one gives the other one up in abandonment just to make the pain stop. You know what is coming. You know how severe the suffering will be. It won't stop until one of you gives in. Your enemy is heartless and relentless. He will stop at nothing to destroy both of you.

So, it begins. You can hear the cries of agony from your lover. You feel the unceasing torment of your own body and mind as you endure for the sake of your one true love. That person is worth it.

Now, take a moment to realize that this is your reality. You have a *real* enemy. He *has* dragged you away from your love— Jesus! Your enemy *has* put you both to the suffering test. He tortured Jesus without mercy and in ways we cannot fathom. He tortures you daily, in every opportunity, and in a variety of ways.

The gut-punch—you're the one who flipped first. You failed your true love. You couldn't withstand the anguish and pain. It was too much. You tapped out. And Jesus? He's still in the other room holding out for the one He loves—you. He breaks over and over again as he bears every new and cruel punishment inflicted on Him. But this isn't even the part that will make your knees drop. That part comes when you find out that He *knows*. He knows you failed. He knows you gave in and left Him there. Even bigger, He knew *before* you ever went in. It changed nothing. His love and faithfulness are not contingent on your strength. His devotion and passion for you never waiver because of your weakness.

See, the thing is, Jesus knows about every failure before it happens; it changes nothing for Him. He doesn't calculate the risk of loving you. He knows the risk, the loss, the whole cost. Knowing all of that, he does not hesitate. He would rather take the torture than not love you.

We often talk about counting the cost to follow Jesus because He asks for our all. If you know where He stands, why would you ever opt-out? Isn't someone who thinks you are worth every single cost worth it themselves?

What does any of this have to do with faith? Everything. If knowing His heart for you doesn't make you want to put every ounce of faith and trust into Him, then I don't have a clue what would. This is a love like no other. You want faith like an unquenchable fire? Start with a passionate love that cannot be broken.

"For love is as strong as death, its jealousy as enduring as the grave. Love flashes like fire, the brightest kind of flame. Many waters cannot quench love, nor can rivers drown it."
Song of Solomon 8:6,7 (NLT)

Reflection and Prayer Focus

We are going to be building on this incredible picture of God's love in the next couple of days and looking at how this relates to our faith in times of tests and trials. Today, pray that the Lord will prepare your heart for growing pains. Ask Him to help you use the times you fall to get back up faster, stronger, and more powerful in spiritual battle.

Personal Notes

Day 7: Warning! He's coming for you

When I say that my faith has been tested over the years, do not imagine I mean it ended with the story of the miscarriage. While that was a painful experience that I cannot do justice with words, I want to tell you about another time I was tested. Last year, at the beginning of 2020 (before anyone knew it was going to be a year to scrap) I was pregnant with our second boy. On January 25th, my water broke at 23 weeks. Through a whirlwind of events, I had an emergency C-section on February 1st and they pulled a lifeless baby from my womb.

Before I tell the climax and the wrap-up of this story, let me backtrack. Literally, the morning before this unfolded, I felt an incredibly clear message from the Lord on my heart. I remember in my devotional time that morning that I kept hearing words of warning. I knew them from somewhere. Luke 22:31, "Indeed, Satan has asked for you, that he may sift you as wheat. But I have prayed for you, that your faith should not fail; and when you have returned to Me, strengthen your brethren." (NKJV) I read it over and over. I wept. I knew He was warning me. I heard His voice loud and clear as He admonished me, *he's coming for you!*

This warning was the one Jesus gave to Peter before he denied Jesus. There is so much girth to this passage I could expand on it for days, but I'll try to condense it. Start with the warning. Notice that this isn't a warning that Satan is going to get you. It's that he is coming to "sift you like wheat" this means to weed out anything extra. This means torture. Test. This likely reminds you of a time in your life you have felt "sifted."

Now, move on to the next part, "but I have prayed for you, that your faith should not fail." Jesus *prays for you*! He is praying that your faith will not fail. Now, this gets interesting because we know that Peter didn't exactly pass the test. At least not the torture test. He *did* pass the faith test. You see, you *will* fail and make mistakes, but that doesn't have to be the death of your faith. Your faith can survive your imperfections. How? It's not about you. It's about Jesus. Jesus knew that Peter would fail in the short-term torture test, but He knew that in the long-term faith test, Peter would make it. Because he had tasted the goodness of God and the incredible love of Jesus. You see the evidence of this as Jesus goes on and says, "and when you have returned to Me, strengthen your brethren." He didn't say *if.* He knew that when someone truly tastes the relentless love of Christ, there is no if to their return. Just when.

Tomorrow I will finish my story and go more in-depth on the "sifting" that happened through this journey. Today, know that Satan is going to sift you. Get ready. Know that through your torture tests, you will have times when you fail. But Jesus has already prayed for you. He knows your faith can survive your falls.

"Dear brothers and sisters, when troubles of any kind come your way, consider it an opportunity for great joy. For you know that when your faith is tested, your endurance has a chance to grow. So let it grow, for when your endurance is fully developed, you will be perfect and complete, needing nothing."
James 1:2-4 (NLT)

Reflection and Prayer Focus

Spend time today asking the Lord to prepare you for the tests you will endure at times. Ask Him to give you the strength to remember His goodness and love when the trials arise. If you're currently facing trials, spend extra time asking Him to help you retrain your mind to consider your trials growth opportunities to love Him fiercely. Every test you go through refines you. If you will choose to grow in the trouble, you will become a mighty force of God's grace—a force to be reckoned with.

Personal Notes

Day 8: Walk in the Fire

Yesterday, I was telling you about the warning I felt in my spirit before being tested in a significant way. As I sat in my hospital room reflecting on the warning, I felt an odd peace. I had no idea what was coming, but I knew it was going to hurt. What I knew most of all, was with Whom I was about to walk into the fire. I had the records. I knew He was trustworthy. He was tortured for me—and He never broke, despite my weakness. The same God of miracles from the Old Testament sat with me then, reminding me that He has always been faithful, always will be faithful, and His love for me is everlasting. He could be trusted.

While my lifeless son was pulled from my womb, I slept under anesthesia. It was okay, God never slept. He was there. He watched the whole thing unfold as the medical staff worked to revive my son. He was there. He was faithful. He was faithful as they put in the effort for fifteen fruitless moments. He was faithful as they decided to call the time of death. He was faithful as they began protocol for the final listen as they record the time on the clock to write on the death certificate. He was faithful as He breathed on my baby boy with the breath of life, causing the final listen to be met with a faint heartbeat. He was faithful in every single moment.

The coming days and felt far less miraculous as my son fought a harrowing battle in the Neonatal Intensive Care Unit for four long months. My faith was tested in ways I never imagined in those days. Some days my son teetered on death. Some days his prognosis was existence, but not life.

In terms of being sifted, Shadrach, Meshach, and Abednego were some men devoted and passionate about their God. When they were caught disobeying a decree to worship the gods of their king, they stood tall. They were about to be burned alive for this grievance. Their response: "If it be so, our God whom we serve is able to rescue us from the furnace of blazing fire; and He will rescue us from your hand, O king. But *even* if He does not, let it be known to you, O king, that we are not going to serve your gods nor worship the golden statue that you have set up." (Daniel 3:16-18,

NASB) I have always loved this encounter because of their incredible position. They were confident God would save them, but *beyond* that was the *knowledge* that even if He had other plans, He could be trusted. He was faithful, and they knew that He was a God with higher thoughts than them. If they couldn't understand the grand plan and it meant their death, so be it. Why? Because the goodness and faithfulness of God were unchanged. Eternity is a much grander view than the picture we have of this life.

The story of Shadrach, Meshach, and Abednego ends with an incredible experience of their God. God didn't rescue them from the fire. They went in the fire, and He wasn't the one to bring them out. Instead, He walked into it with them! The king saw a fourth person walking around with them and they are all four unharmed.

When the torture test comes, choose the fire. It won't seem so intimidating when you know Who you're walking into it with. In pain and in joy, He is good, and He is trustworthy.

"Should we accept only good from God and not adversity?"
Job 2:10 (CSB)

Reflection and Prayer Focus

Hone in on what it means to trust God in the difficulties. Realize that this means a kind of surrender that knows His eternity big picture plan supersedes your comfort in this life, and you can absolutely trust Him to do what is best for you...but He isn't dealing with just this set of circumstances. He's mapping your eternity. Pray about having this kind of trust.

Personal Notes

Day 9: Your View is Important

There are numerous examples in scripture of someone's focus being key. Peter is one that comes to mind. In Matthew 14, when he walked on water toward Jesus, he only sank when he took his eyes off of Jesus. I hope that really gets into your heart. This was a wonderful example of a faith test—how much did Peter trust Jesus? Immensely...while his focus was on him. The second your focus drifts off of Jesus and onto your trial, your shaky situation, your struggle—that's when things get rocky. All of the sudden, you start sinking. Tip: if you're ever in the midst of a trial and you feel yourself sinking, check your view. You can bet you took your eyes off of Jesus. When your eyes are on Him, things might not be easy, but you'll always be on top of the waves, not under them.

Now, be sure and note that when this happened, Peter cried out for Jesus in verse 30, and Jesus saved him. You're going to lose focus sometimes, because, well, you're not perfect. But when we do lose our focus, we must cry out to Jesus. When you do, He will be faithful to rescue you, but it requires refocusing on Him. You can't take His hand of rescue without looking at Him.

Another example of the importance of focus—and one of my personal favorites—is the beautiful story of Stephen, the first martyr of Christ. He was stoned to death for committing the heinous crime of believing that Jesus was Who He claimed to be. After he preached the gospel in response to the accusations brought against him, he looked upward—ever focusing on Jesus—and said, "Look! I see the heavens opened and the Son of Man standing at the right hand of God!" (Acts 7:58 NKJV) When the religious rulers heard this, they charged him, dragged him outside, and stoned him.

During the time stones flew at and crushed his body, scripture records him calling out to Jesus—not to save him, but to receive him. He wasn't worried about getting out of it alive, he was worried about being focused and devoted to the love of his soul. He was so wrapped up in Jesus that he imitated him in death when he, like Jesus, begged for the forgiveness of his offenders. Imagine this kind of laser focus! Your body is literally being destroyed, blow by blow, and your attention is all on Jesus. Your attention is all on His everlasting and unrelenting love and making sure He is revealed to those murdering you.

That is focus! That is a view that shakes heaven and moves mountains. Forget about the miracle, look at Jesus—the miracles surround Him. You get caught up in miracles, you'll probably never see one. You get caught up in Jesus, you'll see many. Your view makes all the difference in whether you sink in the waves or walk on the waves.

"Those who love me, I will deliver; I will protect those who know my name. When they call to me, I will answer them; I will be with them in trouble, I will rescue them and honor them. With long life I will satisfy them, and show them my salvation."
Psalms 91: 14-16 (NRSV)

Reflection and Prayer Focus

Know that as you read the passage for today, the promises of God are often misunderstood and misconstrued to be what we want and mean what we like. Read these promises with an eternal lens as we've been talking about. I challenge you, even dare you, to ask God to start revealing things to you through this lens. See how it changes your perspective about different things.

Personal Notes

Day 10: First Things First

At the end of yesterday's devotion, we briefly touched on the thought that if you focus on miracles they will likely evade you, but if you focus on the Miracle Maker, you will likely see many. This is an absurdly simple, yet often overlooked teaching of scripture. Don't get me wrong, many ministers are doing their due diligence in presenting this concept, but it is far too easy for us to hear it and not consume it. If you were one-hundred-percent honest with yourself, could you truthfully say that you are seeking God's direction before your own desires?

In Matthew 6, Jesus spends some time telling His followers that wherever their treasure is—whatever they prioritize—is where their heart is. He admonishes them to build their treasure in the form of everlasting things. He wanted them—wants *you*—to have their hearts all wrapped up and invested in the things of God. Where is your treasure, and therefore your heart? Is it on earthly things or things beyond this life?

It's terrifyingly easy to focus on us and use God like a vending machine to see our wants and desires come into our lives. Sometimes it is dreams we chase that we ask Him to sanction when He may have an entirely different—and often better—plan! I will admit this has been a weakness of mine as well.

In fact, it has been on my heart a lot lately. When Jesus was twelve, he was separated from his family as they were traveling. When they searched frantically for him, they finally found him in the temple...teaching! At *twelve*! When they started to scold him for not staying with the group, his response is piercing. "Didn't you know I must be about my Father's business?"

It is far too normal—particularly in our culture—to have a habit of asking God to bless our business, but not asking to be about His. Sadly, this way of thinking is plaguing the western Church like a bad stomach bug that won't go away. It has become so normal to think this way that we've developed an immunity to even noticing it. We demand God's blessing and stamp of approval on our endeavors simply because we are His children and entitled to His endorsement. We rarely adopt the heart posture of asking to be endorsable. Rather than racing to God with our next plan and saying, "Sign here," what would happen in our lives if we raced to Him and said, "Where do I sign?" It's serving versus being served. We commonly step over that line and start subconsciously asking God to serve us and our plans rather than asking how we can serve Him. You're not going to wield mighty faith if you're only seeking to be served and blessed.

Faith grows as you become intimate with the One in Whom you place faith. You will never experience that intimacy if you're not taking the time to get close, ask to know Him, and learn how to love Him better.

The blessings do come...when you're following His path. The stamp of approval does come...when you're asking Him to use you how He sees fit. Surrender and devotion are your direct link to divine endorsement.

"But seek first the kingdom of God and His righteousness, and all these things shall be added to you."
Matthew 6:33 (NKJV)

"Commit your actions to the Lord, and your plans will succeed."
Proverbs 16:3 (NLT)

Reflection and Prayer Focus

We've been laying lots of groundwork, and I can't wait to see how God continues to work in our hearts as we go through this study together. As we ponder the things we have covered so far, lean into the concept of simply knowing and loving the Lord intimately. This will be the greatest move you ever make. Intimacy comes from openness and private one-on-one experiences. Begin building on whatever level of intimacy you already have with the Lord. It's only going to get better, and you're only going to see bigger, more amazing things than you imagined.

Personal Notes

Day 11: Active Faith

I love the term active faith. Who wants to have idle faith? It's basically redundant to even say active faith because actual faith is never inactive, but still, I love the term. Perhaps I love this expression because it brings such awareness to faith. You can't maintain fitness if you don't exercise regularly. In the same way, you can't maintain faith that you aren't using. Use it or lose it! Unused faith dies. It cannot exist if it is inactive.

The book of James is one of my favorites of the New Testament. It's beautifully blunt and challenging. I can never get enough of it. It's also a source of discomfort and frustration for many. I've heard countless debates on the whole faith versus works topic. The thing is, I've never understood why there is a debate at all. We live in such a mindset of the Grace Movement that we lose some fundamental truths in the midst of it. There is no greater truth that we are saved through *grace alone*! Likewise, there is no greater truth that when grace actually gets ahold of you, it changes you! When you are intercepted by the renewing and reviving love of God, you cannot remain unchanged. Furthermore, if you continually seek Him, as you are admonished in scripture, you will continually change.

So, when James said in 2:17 that, "So you see, faith by itself isn't enough. Unless it produces good deeds, it is dead and useless." (NLT) His message is very clear and simple. You cannot be saved without faith in Jesus, but saying, "I believe" is not enough! Actually putting your faith in the Lord produces a product that looks an awful lot like His handiwork. You cannot actually trust in Him, love Him, grow intimate with Him and *not* see it produce works. The closer you grow to the Lord, the more your faith in Him grows. The more your faith grows, the more you see opportunities to reflect him. Suddenly you realize you can no longer ignore the needs around you. Saying "God bless you" to those in need stops being enough and you begin to start *being* the blessing! You hear about needs and you go into action to meet them. You hear of hurting people and you run to hold them and love them. You see a hungry person and you go out of your way to feed them. You skip the extra want in your life to offer the need in someone else's.

Want to talk about radical faith that starts to outgrow you? *This* is where it happens. Miracles are what most people want when they talk about faith. Real faith, mature faith, is a desperation to be so in step with Jesus that you become the miracle for someone else. That is what it means to have faith in Jesus. You start turning into His reflection, little by little.

"Now someone may argue, 'Some people have faith; others have good deeds.' But I say, 'How can you show me your faith if you don't have good deeds? I will show you my faith by my good deeds."
James 2:18 (NLT)

"No one lights a lamp and then puts it under a basket. Instead, a lamp is placed on a stand, where it gives light to everyone in the house. In the same way, let your good deeds shine out for all to see, so that everyone will praise your heavenly Father."
Matthew 5:15-16 (NLT)

Reflection and Prayer Focus

It is my hope that you will accept the challenge of today's devotional. Begin to question whether or not your faith is active. Is it really there if there is no evidence of it? If there is evidence, ask for more opportunities to shine it out! When you start asking God for the opportunities to reflect Him and meet the needs of others, you will begin to see God do extraordinary things. This is the kind of request God loves to hear. When you pray this way, you get straight to His heart. See what kind of massive faith God wants to grow in your life.

Personal Notes

Day 12: Faith Breeds Sacrifice

No one likes the word sacrifice. It's intimidating and scary. What if it's required of us? The very definition means something extremely hard. If it weren't difficult, it wouldn't be a sacrifice. No one wants to sacrifice, but everyone wants to be worth sacrificing something for. You might be wondering what any of this has to do with faith. It ties in closely with yesterday's devotion about works. Faith that is wild and powerful is faith that is not only willing but also seeking the opportunity to sacrifice.

Several years ago, I started on a quest—one I'm still on—to learn what sacrifice looks like in my life, and how I can ensure I am living a life of sacrifice. You might question why anyone would want to do this. It's because a life absent of sacrifice is a life of comfort and complacency. If I ever become at home in this world, I have missed the mark of my purpose. I was made for a different world. A redeemed and perfect world where the only thing that satisfies me is the Creator.

You see, sacrifice is all about cost. If you give away something that was free and you don't want, it isn't a sacrifice at all. When you give away something that means something to you, something valuable and important to you, you're sacrificing.

We've been on this path to finding faith. We know it starts with knowing Who we are dealing with. When you know the heart of the One asking for your faith, you know He is trustworthy. When you get to know His heart, you find you start to love Him so deeply. When you love Him, you both want and need more intimacy with Him. When you get to this point, you realize you could never stand the thought of giving Him anything less than your all.

When I first began asking the Lord to move me to sacrifice, I remember it started when the Holy Spirit nudged my heart after reading 2 Samuel 24. In the buildup, David is looking for a place to offer sacrifices to the Lord in worship. He asks a landowner to sell him his field for this purpose. The landowner, knowing David is the king, tries to simply gift David with the land, as well as the animals for the sacrifice. David's response in verse 24 hit a nerve in my heart that has never recovered. "No, I insist on buying it from you for a price, for I will not offer to the Lord my God burnt offerings that cost me nothing." (HCSB) I still get all worked up every time I read this. It hit me then and there that I never want to be so shallow in my faith and devotion to the Lord that I would offer him a sacrifice, a praise, a life, an offering of any sort that cost me nothing at all. He gave me everything, sacrificing His all. It cost Him everything! Let me never be guilty of offering Him anything that doesn't cost me something.

"Therefore, brothers and sisters, in view of the mercies of God, I urge you to present your bodies as a living sacrifice, holy and pleasing to God; this is your true worship. Do not be conformed to this age, but be transformed by the renewing of your mind, so that you may discern what is the good, pleasing, and perfect will of God."
Romans 12:1-2 (CSB)

Reflection and Prayer Focus

I challenge you to begin the same quest I started some years ago. Begin asking the Lord to show you what sacrifice looks like in your life, and commit to never offering Him anything that costs you nothing. Pray that he will prepare your heart for the upcoming days and the things He has yet to speak to you. Ask Him to help you be open and ready to allow Him to rearrange your heart and mind as you seek to grow.

Personal Notes

Day 13: What is Your Sacrifice?

Yesterday we talked a little about sacrifice. There are a whole host of ways the Lord might lead you to sacrifice in your life. Seek direction to find the right way for you to sacrifice. First, know that your sacrifice will look different in different seasons of your life. Second, know that it will not be something easy. That's the point. If you're unwilling to sacrifice in an area of your life, it needs to be the first one you tackle. Anything you're that entangled with is the very reason you need to give it up. Your heart lives with your treasure, remember? If you're unwilling to give something up, you're walking on the property lines of idolatry. I know this hurts. I've had to identify some areas in my own life like this. The goal is to reach a point where the only thing in your life you refuse to sacrifice is your devotion to the King of Kings.

Another way of sacrifice is service. When you're willing to serve others, you're stepping into Jesus's backyard. This is where He lives—in service to others.

Truthfully, serving others is a breeding ground for great faith. You might think that sounds odd, but believe me, when you serve others as Jesus served, you will begin to love and pray for others in bold ways. You will learn to trust the Lord with those you love. You will see His faithfulness in this area and you will see God work in mighty ways.

Sometimes sacrificing through serving might look like giving money, (the thing we all tend to think of) but often it looks like time and actions. Sometimes it is putting yourself on hold for the sake of others. We live in a world that glorifies putting yourself first and making sure you invest in people that invest in you. I have often seen the act of doing for others who would do nothing for you referred to as a "toxic" trait. No! Please, please hear me! Choosing who you invest in based on this merit is a toxic trait! We aren't supposed to operate this way, loved ones! We are supposed to look different than the world.

Invest in the one who will give nothing back. Pitch in at church or volunteer at a local charity. Give up your plans once in a while to do something for others in your life. Put yourself in an uncomfortable position from time to time! We have to abandon the self-serving mentality of the world and adopt the self-denying giving mentality of Jesus.

Judas betrayed Jesus, and yet Jesus washed his feet along with the rest of the disciples. IT wasn't a secret to Jesus that Judas was going to betray Him, and it changed nothing. If Jesus was willing to serve and invest in Judas, how much more should we be willing to serve and invest in anyone and everyone that Jesus sends our way. Know that there are appropriate ways of serving, and that service doesn't mean self-deprecation or putting yourself in bad or cyclical situations. Serving others in a healthy way is doing what you can and putting the tools in their reach to continue on. It also means continuing to meet them with the Love of Jesus, no matter what.

"Let each of you look not to your own interests, but to the interests of others. Let the same mind be in you that was in Christ Jesus, who, though he was in the form of God, did not regard equality with God as something to be exploited, but emptied himself, taking the form of a slave, being born in human likeness. And being found in human form, he humbled himself and became obedient to the point of death—even death on a cross."
James 2:18 (NRSV)

Reflection and Prayer Focus

Prayerfully reflect on the areas of your life where God would have you sacrifice. Also, consider how you can live a life of service and resemble Jesus in this way. Ask the Lord to show you proverbial feet to wash. Just as He washed the feet of all of those with Him, ask Him to open your eyes to ways you can serve and love others. You can bet this will cause your faith to blossom and you will see incredible things begin to happen around you.

Personal Notes

Day 14: Knowing the Cost

On day 6, there was a brief mention of counting the cost of following Jesus. There is so much I could say here. I could tell you to consider the cost of not following Him. I could tell you, as I have, to look at what you cost Him, and how He still chose you. However, I would be remiss if I did not discuss the actual cost of having a ground-shaking faith in the God of the Universe. It isn't cheap, and it isn't painless. It's hard, gritty, painful, exhausting, and costly. It is worth it.

There are days when it will feel like the world is against you. Unfortunately, it is. Jesus tells us to be prepared for such a thing. He is quite transparent about how hard it is to follow Him. He makes it no secret how sacrificial we must be. When you follow Jesus, you're bound to lose friends. Now, I know that for some of you that seems extreme because your friends are Christians. Hear me clearly: there is a difference between professing salvation and following Jesus. I'm talking about trekking across dangerous grounds, making decisions that sometimes don't make sense. I'm talking about giving up opportunities that look perfect in order to choose something that looks lesser. This is a radical change in your life we are talking about. We are discussing looking at things through different lenses. I always like to say we look, hear, and speak through the filter of the Holy Spirit when we are walking with Jesus.

You'll know you're walking with Jesus when your view starts to change and people start to look at you like you're a little kooky when it comes to following the Lord. Now, understand that the Lord did not call us to be weirdos and nut jobs. He *did* call us and even ordain us by His Spirit to follow a path foreign to this world. We do not live by the rules of this world, we live by the rules of God. We don't look to justify our actions by worldly standards. We strive to humbly submit to the will of God, even when it is uncomfortable.

As I said, you will lose friends. Even some of your Christian friends will look at you like you've lost it when your goals start to look a lot less like the American dream and start to resemble following the trail of a nomadic dust-covered carpenter. When you begin to tie your dreams to eternity rather than retirement, your life transforms in a wild and beautiful way.

Another thing I always say: Following Jesus is the greatest adventure you'll ever go on. Many people have looked at me like I was a wacko when they've heard me say this. My husband even thought it was an odd saying many years ago when we met. Now, he says it himself. Why? Because he's been on the adventure! He's still traveling those winding and unpredictable roads. He's stepped into uncertain terrain and seen the reward, the beauty, and the unceasing love of Christ leading the way. Jesus has never led us on a boring journey. Remember, professing salvation is one thing. You can live a boring church pew life that way. *Following* Jesus on the other hand, means waltzing right into war zones, be they real or spiritual. It will never be dull. It will never be predictable. It will always lead you into places of trust. It will bring you face to face with hurting people and serious needs. It will equip you to be used. It will never leave you the same. You know the cost. Is it worth it?

"And whoever does not bear his cross and come after Me cannot be My disciple. For which of you, intending to build a tower, does not sit down first and count the cost, whether he has enough to finish it."
Luke 14:27-28 (NKJV)

Reflection and Prayer Focus

Do an exercise with me. Write your name on the blank spot and then read it aloud. Then, pray diligently about it. Consider carefully the cost of total self-abandon. When you're ready, answer the question with the most honest position you can possibly take. Jesus never offered the illusion that following Him in this life would be easy or low cost. He wants you to know what you're getting into when you choose Him, and once you know it all, he asks _____, *will you follow me, **wherever I** go?*

Personal Notes

Day 15: Standing Alone

In the sixth chapter of John, Jesus had just finished saying some pretty difficult to swallow and understand things. The people's response? They left.

Yesterday, we talked about knowing the cost before embarking on the journey. Many of these people clearly did not know the cost before they started to follow Jesus. That is why they walked away, right? Not entirely. You see, if you're all in, totally in love and devoted, the cost is not the issue. Sure, you feel the cost, but it doesn't deter you and send you back the direction you came. If you find yourself slinking back home—metaphorically—because the cost was too great, you have misunderstood your own heart. The cost was not the root issue. The cost was only too great because you were not fully invested in the One Who loves you more than His own body. When you surrender to Love Himself and become so wrapped up in Him that He is where your life begins and ends, the cost will not be too great.

When Jesus saw all of these people giving up on Him and walking back, his heart ached. If only they knew how He loved them. Scripture says He looked to His remaining twelve disciples and asked them, "Do you also want to go away?" (v. 67) The wonderful response of Peter in this story is one I hold close to my own heart and have recited in many dark moments when the enemy says, "time to abandon ship!" I can't presume to know exactly what Peter was thinking, but I feel that it was surely proceeded by a quick examination of his life after which he concluded that following Jesus _was_ his life. So, he spoke up and answered, "Lord, to whom shall we go? You have the words of eternal life. Also, we have come to believe and know that You are the Christ, the Son of the living God." (v. 68, 69) I love his answer. When you are in the midst of brokenness, the enemy will always whisper words of abandonment to you. When tests and trials hit, Jesus will ask you, "Do you want to leave too?" We must strive to be in a place where our only response can be, "Where else would I go? I know who you are! There is nothing else."

Your friends and family will sometimes turn around. Ministers you look up to will occasionally turn around. Those you think have all the faith in the world will turn around. Don't turn with them. Keep your eyes on Him. Know Who He is at all times. Love Him deeply. When everyone else turns around, keep following.

"And if it is evil in your eyes to serve the Lord, choose this day whom you will serve, whether the gods your fathers served in the region beyond the River, or the gods of the Amorites in whose land you dwell. But as for me and my house, we will serve the Lord."
Joshua 24:15 (ESV)

Reflection and Prayer Focus

Take a good look at the world around you. You will at some point find yourself standing alone when it comes to serving the Lord. Follow Him anyway. Pray for strength to do so and the strength and grace to keep your eyes on Him in order to do so. In addition, list three to five people you know that you can pray the same way for today. The hurting world needs believers who will follow Jesus no matter what. Those are the people who leave a mark on the world for Jesus. Be one of those, and pray for others to be empowered to be so as well.

Personal Notes

Day 16: Praying for Increase

If I have heard it once, I have heard it a thousand times. "Don't pray for an increase in faith. You know what will happen when you do. You'll be put to the test!" *So what?!* So many Christians say this and see no problem with it. I have to admit that this absolutely frustrates me. We are crippling other believers this way! How could we ever be so blatant as to tell someone not to pursue faith? This minimizes faith and sends a message that we should be content with small and wimpy faith so that we can avoid pain and difficulty. The thought is that if we ask for an increase, we are inviting tests and trials. Suppose this is true. Is that so bad? Isn't the end result worth it? This reasoning is like saying that we shouldn't resolve to get fit because it will mean we have to hit the gym or start that new diet. Okay, those things might not be fun, but they yield the results that make it worthwhile. What kind of weak Church are we fostering when our kneejerk reaction is "don't ask for the increase!"

The disciples asked Jesus to increase their faith because they realized that the things Jesus was asking them to do and be were far beyond their own abilities. Jesus answered by telling them that a tiny amount of faith would suffice. He then goes on to talk about something that seems unrelated...except it isn't. He tells them about how faithful servants will give glory to their master when they have done their job, saying they've only done what was asked of them. The point? It's not about *their* faith. It's about *Jesus!* Everything He asks us to do and be *is* outside of our abilities. That's the point. We can only accomplish it through Him.

So, what is an increase in faith? It's an increase in Jesus. An increase in loving Him. Do trials come when you ask for the increase? Maybe. Probably. Because the enemy hates the idea of you having more of Jesus. He will hinder you at every corner if he thinks he has a shot at making you turn around and go back. The important thing to remember is that you can let go of everything except Jesus in these trials. When they come, hold fast to Him because He is the One Who will overcome them. You don't have to. He already has.

Fear says to avoid the trials. Complacency says don't experience discomfort. Be brave enough to ask for the increase!

"The apostles said to the Lord, 'Increase our faith!' And the Lord said, "If you had faith like a grain of mustard seed, you could say to this mulberry tree, 'Be uprooted and planted in the sea,' and it would obey you."
Luke 17:5-6 (ESV)

"I have told you these things so that in me you may have peace. You will have suffering in this world. Be courageous! I have conquered the world."
John 16:33 (CSB)

Reflection and Prayer Focus

Challenge yourself this week to pray for an increase in your faith. Ask for an increase of Jesus. That means surrendering to Him and asking Him to rearrange your heart. Ask to have more of His anointing and His Spirit at work in your life. Are you ready for the increase? Ask for it!

Personal Notes

Day 17: Big Faith vs. Little Faith

Sometimes we have a tendency to get caught up in the idea of the size of faith. Do we have big faith or a little faith? We disassembled a little of that yesterday when we talked about the increase being less about faith than it is about Jesus. This very book is titled Faith Bigger than Me. I want to unpack that. It is not meant to implicate that your faith is huge but rather that your faith and dedication to Jesus consumes you! The deeper you go with the Lord the more you disappear in many ways. In other ways, you finally appear—more vibrant than ever. The real point though is not about the size, but about the existence of it! If you truly have real faith in Jesus, where you choose Him, knowing the cost, ready to face it all, your faith consumes you, because He consumes you. Your faith becomes bigger than you when you fade away into Him.

In Luke chapter nine, there is a story of an epileptic boy being brought to Jesus to be healed. Reportedly, the disciples had tried to heal the boy and couldn't. Let me pause for a moment to mention that in scripture, infirmities and illnesses of varying kinds were often referred to as spirits or demons. Back to the story—when they brought the boy to Jesus and told him that they had been unsuccessful, he shows displeasure, to the point he calls them an "unbelieving and perverse generation." Sounds like harsh language, right? Why would he be so upset? If you will go back you will notice that earlier in the same chapter is where we find Jesus talking about counting the cost and taking up the cross. He has *just* been explaining what it means to be all in when you follow Him. Then, here comes His closest followers to report that they failed to heal this boy. What is the implication?

The same story is found in Matthew chapter seventeen. In verse nineteen the disciples ask Jesus why they were unable to accomplish this healing. In verse twenty, He answers them, "Because of your little faith,' he told them, 'For truly I tell you, if you have faith the size of a mustard seed, you will tell this mountain, "Move from here to there," and it will move. Nothing will be impossible for you." (CSB) Ouch. After all this, the disciples still didn't have big enough faith...but again, we misunderstand. The issue is not the *size* of your faith, it is the existence of your faith. The implication was the lack of faith altogether. You see, the mustard seed is tiny. Jesus wasn't using this as an actual size standard, but rather an illustration for two things. The first is that the very existence of faith at any level is enough. The second illustration comes when you realize that the mustard seed, while deficient in size will grow aggressively, without allowing itself to be impeded, until it becomes a whole tree.

How *big* your faith is doesn't matter. The existence of it is all that Jesus is concerned with. Why? Because once it exists, it's exposed to Him, and He will make it grow like a wildfire that can't be quenched.

So, dear reader, have a little faith.

"And my righteous ones will live by faith. But I will take no pleasure in anyone who turns away."
Hebrews 10:38 (NLT)

Reflection and Prayer Focus

When my son was in the neonatal intensive care unit, he began having uncontrollable seizures. The medical staff tried various cocktails of medicine to get them under control. The final straw for me sent me digging into the word looking for the story of the epileptic boy. The same story is also found in Mark nine. The Holy Spirit led me there and impressed upon me to consider verse twenty-nine. There, Jesus said to the disciples, "This kind can come out by nothing but prayer and fasting." We began fasting immediately. The seizures stopped. Faith in action is God's Word in action. Pray about how you can employ faith today by tapping into God's Word.

Personal Notes

Day 18: Powerful Faith

Most of us think of miracles galore when we think of powerful faith. In fact, most of us look to grow our faith so that we can see more miracles. Miracles are great! We should want to see more of them. However, that should not be our endgame goal. This shouldn't even be the main motivator for faith. As I've stated, faith is about Jesus. It's all about choosing Him and trusting Him. Miracles are the byproduct of an incredible relationship with God.

In fact, in Luke chapter ten, the disciples have begun to see these byproducts. They come back to Jesus astounded at these byproducts. They are elated that they have such power to make miraculous things happen by their faith. Yet, once again, they—like us—get a little caught up in the miracle part of it. Jesus cautions them about it and draws their focus back to what is important. He reiterates that yes, He has given them the power to do these things, but that cannot be their focus or source of joy. His words are, "However, don't rejoice that the spirits submit to you, but rejoice that your names are written in heaven." (Luke 10:20, HCSB) See what He's getting at? If you're chasing miracles, you're going to end up falling and turning around, because you've taken your eyes off of Him. Keep your eyes on what matters—your relationship with Jesus. Eternity is the prize.

Don't fall into the trap of distraction. Your faith will lose its power when you take your eyes off of the source of your power. The *only* way to have powerful faith is to be immersed in the Holy Spirit of God and so focused on Him that He colors everything you do.

If you want to have powerful faith, have a powerful love for the King of Kings. Love Him so much that you start to sound like Him, look like Him, walk like Him, and love like Him. When you meet the broken, nothing will happen. When Jesus meets the broken, He doesn't leave it that way. Be the route by which Jesus meets the brokenness around you and begins to put things back together. Miracles become a common occurrence when you stay in close contact with the One Who manufactures them. That being said, when your eyes are squarely on Him, you will always be more excited by Him than the miracles.

Powerful faith tells the world that there is One Who heals. You become the mouthpiece. Furthermore, you're not alone. The Church is made up of people who have chosen Jesus, resolved to follow Him into the desolate places to bring life to the lifeless. Powerful faith will not send you acting alone. It will unite you with Christ and not only will you be connected to Him in an extraordinary way, but you will also be connected to others who love Him just as dearly. A connection like that will see incredible things take place. Imagine the world awakening to the love of God because you and others like you stepped up to follow Jesus in a very real way. *That* is powerful faith!

"For I am not ashamed of the gospel, because it is the power of God that brings salvation to everyone who believes: first to the Jew, then to the Gentile. For in the gospel the righteousness of God is revealed—a righteousness that is by faith from first to last, just as it is written: 'The righteous will live by faith."
Romans 1:16-17 (NIV)

Reflection and Prayer Focus

Being wildly in love with Jesus means being wildly on fire for Him. It means loving the lost rather than resenting them. It means hurting on behalf of the broken and the angry souls around you. People who would offend you become those you shed tears over. The rules are different when you walk in the footsteps of Jesus. You don't give up on those who are labeled as trouble. You fight for them through prayer and love them with *His* love, not yours—your love, and mine, are deeply flawed, His is perfect. Today, ask the Lord to give you powerful faith by starting with the opening of your eyes to see people and love them the way He does. Pray that you will not see them as their sin, their mental state, or their political affiliation, but as the beautiful remnants of what God intended them to be. Then, reach out and help them see Jesus.

Personal Notes

Day 19: Raising the Dead

Now, on to the miracles! When you find yourself so deeply in love with the Lord, the miracles start happening. They stop being such an anomaly and things just happen. The fingerprints of God are all over your life and the evidence of His involvement is in everything. Sometimes it will be blessings that surprise you. Sometimes it will actually be the dead being raised.

As I shared on day eight, my son was God's miraculous hand at work. He was born dead and God breathed into him, raising his tiny body back to life. Our faith saw us through so much during those awful months of his hospital stay. The boy he is now doesn't match the medical charts from those days. He continues to grow and improve, becoming the child God intended.

Faith that is rooted in Jesus will cause you to see those who have no chance at life living full years. It will have severed relationships repaired. It will have the lost causes preaching the gospel. It will have drug addicts recovered and healthy. It will have the alcoholics sober and happy. It will have the promiscuous modest and virtuous. It will have the self-mutilating and desensitized experiencing deep feelings of satisfaction and fulfillment. Faith will see Jesus fix what is broken. These are the greatest miracles you will ever see. If you're hoping for actual rock mountains to fall into the sea, you're after the wrong stuff. Be interested in seeing the chains of mental and emotional captivity fall off of their victims. How do you see those things? See Jesus! Look at Him and He will be your lens to see everything else. Through you, he will rescue the abuse victim, the suicidal, the secret addict, and the shattered person with no direction. These are miracles worth seeing because this is evidence of others seeing that same Jesus.

Are you ready to raise the dead—spiritually or physically? He can do both. Which one is the bigger miracle? Jesus touches on this in Matthew nine, when he tells a crippled man that his sins are forgiven—indicative of spiritual healing, restoration, and reconciliation. The religious leaders raise their eyebrows and get all huffy about it. Why? Because only God can do that. Exactly!

So, Jesus says, "Which is easier: to say, 'Your sins are forgiven,' or to say, 'Get up and walk'? But I want you to know that the Son of Man has authority on earth to forgive sins.' So he said to the paralyzed man, 'Get up, take your man and go home'." (v. 5-7) Do you see what is happening here? The miracle becomes the byproduct. It is simply the outward evidence and manifestation of what God is doing inwardly. So, what is the easier miracle: the visible sign or the inward restoration?

The miracle you're shooting for when you walk with Jesus is the miracle of salvation and restoration of the broken. Guess what? You can and will see both kinds of miracles when you're walking with Jesus! Want to know how I know? Because of Romans 8:11: "And just as God raised Christ Jesus from the dead, he will give life to your mortal bodies by this same Spirit living within you." (NLT) You have the *same* Spirit living within you.

"The Spirit of the Sovereign Lord is upon me, for the Lord has anointed me to bring good news to the poor. He has sent me to comfort the brokenhearted and to proclaim that captives will be released and prisoners will be freed."
Isaiah 61:1 (NLT)

Reflection and Prayer Focus

Lean into the opportunity to be a part of what the Lord wants to do in others. Ask the Lord to show you your mission field. He will be faithful to give you one when you ask. Pray for a vision and a heart to reach those He will send you to. *This* is faith in action!

Personal Notes

Day 20: Great Faith Giants

During one of the darkest and more trial-ridden days of our journey, I stared into the mirror at my own reflection. I had received message after message from people telling me how awesome and amazing my faith was. Yet, here I was, broken and so...human. I saw no strength looking back at me in that mirror. I thought of many "giants of the faith" who had come before me. Many men and women I had read about or heard stories of who had faced horrific trials and stood with great poise, staring fear, pain, and defeat in the face with a heart full of unbreakable faith. Oh, to be like one of them. I wanted to be like them. I looked at my tired and worn face. Nothing. I saw no greatness. I whispered into the air, hoping the Lord was near to listen, "I don't know how to be a giant of the faith. My faith is not amazing. My faith is pathetic and weak." I cracked and the tears flowed. At that moment, I felt the Holy Spirit whisper back, *So was theirs.* What? *It was me. It was my strength that gave them faith. It was always me.*

That was a paramount moment for me in my walk with Jesus. Things did not get easier from there, but from there I knew something in my soul that I had not fully grasped before. I didn't have to have amazing strength and faith. I had to have Him, love Him relentlessly, and follow Him anywhere. He asks us to have faith, but the real and beautiful mystery of it is that He Himself empowers us to have that faith! All we really have to do is choose Him wholly, and constantly. Great faith is not a mighty feeling or empowered emotion. It is choosing Jesus again, and again.

Your very ability to have faith is rooted in His strength, not yours. When you put your faith in Him, He actually gives you the power to maintain it! Our ability to withstand the torture test is never ours—it's His!

I share here a snippet from something I wrote after my mirror moment:

...our display of faith really comes back to Him and only Him! If there is anything good or strong in us,

I assure you it is not us, but Him in us! The truth is, my faith is not amazing. My faith is pathetic. To say otherwise would be to accept some tiny bit of glory and that doesn't belong to me. It ALL belongs to Him. Without His grace, I could have no faith. I am deeply flawed and very frail. I serve a God Who is everything perfect and strong. He has proven Himself good and faithful time and time again since the world began. He has proven Himself good and faithful in my personal life, time and time again. Through happiness, He has been there. Through pain, He has been there. Through tragedy, He has been there. Through my failure, He has been there. How foolish I would be not to choose to trust and believe Him through everything. It is not my strength that drives my faith. It is His unrelenting goodness. It is Him. Only Him.

"My grace is sufficient for you, for My strength is made perfect in weakness."
II Corinthians 12:9 (NKJV)

Reflection and Prayer Focus

The only faith giant is Jesus. Ask Him to help you lean into His strength rather than your own. Psalm 73:26 says, "My flesh and heart may fail; But God is the strength of my heart and my portion forever." (NKJV) We are weak and incapable without His great mercy and strength. When we recognize this, and begin to focus on His strengths instead of our weaknesses, we will find we can withstand things we never imagined, and come out on top. Surrender your weakness today in prayer and ask Him to replace it with His strength.

Personal Notes

Day 21: Boldness and Acceptance

You've made it all the way through our brief journey together. I hope and pray that this is just the beginning of new and amazing depths of your journey with Christ. You see, an amazing thing about following Jesus is that you'll never run out of depths to explore. You can always learn more, grow deeper, and continue to change. He has a unique way of giving us new dreams, bigger plans, and mightier victories than we have the capacity to imagine on our own.

Faith never stops growing. I can't wait for the next depth He will take me to. Over the last year, I've learned much. I've found a boldness in my faith that I did not know before. It is not my boldness. It is His. It has given me the boldness to let go of things that held me back. It has given me the boldness to look beyond the dreams I held so tightly. It has given me the boldness to see bigger and better things that God has for me. It has given me the boldness to go after them.

None of that boldness can come without acceptance first. We have to accept that He is the leader of our trek, not us. We have to accept His map, rather than our own. We have to accept His dreams for us—they're bigger than ours anyway—so they become ours.

When you accept all that we have covered over the last twenty days, you will see boldness overtake you and propel you into some exciting places. It will take you to difficult places. You will still go readily. Because you know Who you're with.

With that boldness, you will see miracles of all shapes and sizes, because you have faith bigger than yourself—a faith-seed turned tree by the One Who perfects your faith. You will fade away into His amazing grace, as you simultaneously find Who you were always meant to be.

Ready—to see what God does with your faith in action?

Set—your eyes on Him!

Go!—*"and make disciples of all nations, baptizing them in the name of the Father and of the Son and the Holy Spirit,*

89

and teaching them to obey everything I have commanded you.
And surely I am with you always to the very end of the age."
Matthew 28:19-20 (NIV)

Reflection and Prayer Focus

Today, I hope you will pray that the Lord will help you to continue your journey of faith. I hope this book has served as a tool that will challenge you and cause you to seek the Lord in a more intense way than you ever have. I also want to ask you the same three questions from the intro of this book.

Question number one: Do you want this?
Do you really want to see your faith grow bigger than you? If you can honestly say yes, they answer the next question.

Question number two: Why? Why do you want stronger faith?
Find the answer that you wrote down before and see if it matches the one you just gave.

Question number three: How will your life change if your faith grows?

I sincerely hope and pray that your questions look different in some way after reading this book and praying through these prompts. Whether your whole perspective changed or you simply gained new insight, it is my heart's desire that the Lord uses this devotional experience to work in your life and do new and wonderful things in and through you.

Personal Notes

ABOUT THE AUTHOR

 Abigail Judith Hall Abigail is a wife, a mother of two, and a lover of the written word. Abigail attended college through Liberty University, studying Psychology and Christian Counseling while her husband served in the U.S. Army. She has lived in Kentucky, Florida, and Hawaii. During her time in Hawaii, Abigail wrote several articles for the Footsteps in Faith section of the Hawaii Army Weekly newspaper. She and her husband now serve as co-youth pastors at their home church in Paducah Kentucky.

In addition to this devotional, Abigail has authored five creative works including, War of Redemption: Awakening Warriors – An allegorical fantasy novel, written under her own name—three children's books, and a mystery novella written under the pseudonym, A.J. Tedford.

Want to know more about our NICU story?

Visit our Facebook blog page Born to Live: Joash's Journey, detailing our youngest son's miraculous scrap with death at birth and his continuing hurdles as he repeatedly defies the odds.

68751672R00056